j 598

Stefoff, Rebecca.
The bird class.
2008.

The Bird Class

The Bird Class

REBECCA STEFOFF

 **Marshall Cavendish**
Benchmark
New York

For my bird-loving friends Kathleen Worley and David Heath

Marshall Cavendish Benchmark
99 White Plains Road
Tarrytown, New York 10591-9001
www.marshallcavendish.us
Text copyright © 2008 by Rebecca Stefoff
Illustrations copyright © 2008 by Marshall Cavendish Corporation
Illustrations by Robert Romagnoli

All Web sites were available and accurate when this book was sent to press.

Editor: Karen Ang
Publisher: Michelle Bisson
Art Director: Anahid Hamparian
Series Designer: Patrice Sheridan

Library of Congress Cataloging-in-Publication Data

Stefoff, Rebecca, date
The Bird class / Rebecca Stefoff. -- 1st ed.
p. cm. -- (Family trees)
Summary: "Explores the habitats, life cycles, and other characteristics of organisms in the bird class"-- Provided by publisher.
Includes bibliographical references and index.
ISBN 978-0-7614-2693-6
1. Birds--Juvenile literature. I. Title. II. Series.

QL676.2.S724 2007
598--dc22

2007007706

Front cover: A peacock.
Title page: Penguins
Back cover: A male masked weaver fashions a sturdy hanging nest from strips of vegetation. The males build these nests, usually in colonies, to attract females.
Page 7: A kingfisher; Page 19: An osprey; Page 33: A hummingbird; Page 59: A gyrfalcon; Page 75: A brown pelican.

Photo research by Candlepants, Incorporated
Front cover credit: Brand X / SuperStock

The photographs in this book are used by permission and through the courtesy of: *Marshall Cavendish Image Library:* 3, 7, 19, 33, 37, 47, 54, 59, 61,75. *Minden Pictures:* Michael Durham, 6; Tui de Roy, 40, 53, 58, 66, 77; Gerry Ellis, 42; Tom Vezo, 43, 49, 56, 72; Pete Oxford, 45, 48; Michael & Patricia Fogden, 46; Mitsuaki Iwago, 68; Michael Quinton, 70; Frans Lanting, 78. *Photo Researchers Inc.:* George Bernard, 9; Science Source, 11; Gerald C. Kelley, 32; Tom McHugh, 80. *Corbis:* Layne Kennedy, 18, 21; Academy of Natural Sciences of Philadelphia, 81. *Natural History Museum, London:* NHML Geological Museum of China/NHMPL, 23, 27. *Mick Ellison:* 25(left and right). *Peter Arnold Inc.:* Bios Gunther Michel, 28; Luiz C. Marigo, 35. *Visuals Unlimited:* Theo Allofs, 36; Arthur Morris, 44, 63, 83; Steve Maslowski, 51, 69; Dwspl, 67. *Animals Animals:* Jennifer Loomis, 38; John Gerlach, 79; Juergen & Christine Sohns, back cover. *Getty Images:* Tim Tietz, 41. *Super Stock:* James Urbach, 50; Steve Vidler, 74. *Shutterstock:* Ronnie Howard, 55; Tim Zurowski, 73. *AP Images:* Saurabh Das, 76.

Printed in Malaysia

3 5 6 4 2

CONTENTS

The common barn owl is one of the world's most adaptable and widespread birds. Folk tales link the owl with spirits of the dead, perhaps because of its mournful-looking face and the white undersides of its wings.

Classifying Life

When most people think of birds, they think of flight. They picture a hummingbird hovering in front of a flower, a flock of swallows circling against the sunset, or a lone eagle soaring above the treetops. The vision of flying like a bird has thrilled and inspired people since ancient times.

Not all birds fly, but most do. Birds' flight is made possible by a set of physical features, such as lightweight skeletons, that they inherited from their ancestors—the dinosaurs. Birds and dinosaurs are not the same, of course. A black-capped chickadee pecking at the sunflower seeds in a backyard birdfeeder is not exactly a *T. rex*. But birds are *T. rex*'s closest living relatives. Nearly all biologists today think that birds are the sole survivors of a large group of animals that once included all the dinosaurs. Dinosaurs became extinct millions of years ago, but the birds remained, and today they are found all over the world.

Amazingly adaptable, birds live in a vast variety of habitats, including some extreme conditions. Some birds, such as the emperor penguin, can even survive the brutal cold of winter in Antarctica. Other kinds of birds flourish in tropical rain forests, scorching deserts, craggy mountain ranges, urban cityscapes, and the skies above the open ocean. Nearly

10,000 species of birds exist around the world today. To understand birds' place in the natural world, and why some scientists call birds the only living dinosaurs, it helps to know something about how scientists classify living things.

THE INVENTION OF TAXONOMY

Science gives us tools for making sense of the natural world. One of the most powerful tools is classification, which means organizing things in a pattern according to their differences and similarities. Since ancient times, scientists who study living things have been developing a classification system for living things. This system is called taxonomy. Scientists use taxonomy to group together organisms that share features, setting them apart from other organisms with different features.

Taxonomy is hierarchical, which means that it is arranged in levels. The highest levels are categories that include many kinds of organisms. These large categories are divided into smaller categories, which in turn are divided into still smaller ones. The most basic category is the species, a single kind of organism.

The idea behind taxonomy is simple, but the world of living things is complex and full of surprises. Taxonomy is not a fixed pattern. It keeps changing to reflect new knowledge or ideas. Over time, scientists have developed rules for adjusting the pattern even when they disagree on the details.

One of the first taxonomists was the ancient Greek philosopher Aristotle (384-322 BCE), who investigated many branches of science, including biology. Aristotle arranged living things on a sort of ladder, or scale. At the bottom were those he considered lowest, or least developed, such as worms. Above them were things he considered higher, or more developed, such as fish, then birds, then mammals.

For centuries after Aristotle, taxonomy made little progress. People who studied nature tended to group organisms together by features that were easy to see, such as separating trees from grasses or birds from fish. However, they did not try to develop a system for classifying all life. Then, between 1682 and 1705, an English naturalist named John Ray published a plan of the living world that was designed to have a place for every species of plant and animal. Ray's system was hierarchical, with several levels of larger and smaller categories. It was the foundation of modern taxonomy.

Swedish naturalist Carolus Linnaeus (1707-1778) built on that foundation to create the taxonomic system used today. Linnaeus was chiefly interested in plants, but his system of classification included all living things. Its highest level of classification was the kingdom. To Linnaeus, everything belonged to either the plant kingdom or the animal kingdom. Each of these kingdoms was divided into a number of smaller categories called classes. Each class was divided into orders. Each order was divided into genera. Each genus (the singular form of genera) contained one or more species.

The northern gannet is called *Anser bassanus* in this 1684 drawing, but other scientists at the time may have had completely different names for it. After Linnaeus revolutionized scientific naming, however, the bird was known to all as *Morus bassanus*.

Linnaeus also developed another of Ray's ideas, a method for naming species. Before Linnaeus published his important work *System of Nature* in 1735, scientists had no recognized system for referring to plants and animals. Organisms were generally known by their common names, but many of them had different names in various countries. As a result, two naturalists might call the same plant or animal by two different names—or use the same name for two different organisms. Linnaeus wanted to end such confusion, so that scholars everywhere could communicate clearly about plants and animals. He started the practice of giving each plant or animal a two-part scientific name made up of its genus and species. These names were in Latin, the scientific language of Linnaeus's day. For example, the stubby-legged, crested bird commonly known as the rockhopper penguin has the scientific name *Eudyptes chrysocome* (or *E. chrysocome* after the first time the full name is used). This bird belongs to the genus *Eudyptes,* a name that means "good diver" in Latin. The genus *Eudyptes* contains six kinds of penguins, but the rockhopper is set apart from the other five by the second part of its name, *chrysocome.* That name refers only to the rockhopper penguin.

Linnaeus named hundreds of species. Other scientists quickly adopted his highly flexible system to name many more. The Linnaean system appeared at a time when European naturalists were exploring the rest of the world, finding thousands of new plants and animals. This flood of discoveries was overwhelming at times, but Linnaean taxonomy helped scientists identify and organize their finds.

TAXONOMY TODAY

Biologists still use the system of scientific naming that Linnaeus developed (anyone who discovers a new species can choose its scientific name, which is in Latin, or once in a while in Greek). Other aspects of taxonomy, though, have changed since Linnaeus's time.

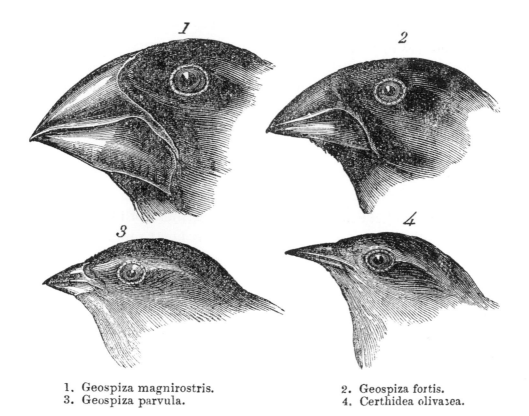

1. Geospiza magnirostris.
3. Geospiza parvula.

2. Geospiza fortis.
4. Certhidea olivaᴣea.

These four species of finches from the Galapagos Islands descended from the same ancestral species. Studying the related forms of these finches and other creatures led Charles Darwin to the discovery of evolution.

Over the years, as biologists learned more about the similarities and differences among living things, they added new levels to taxonomy. Eventually, an organism's full classification could include the following taxonomic levels: kingdom, subkingdom, phylum (some biologists use division instead of phylum for plants and fungi), subphylum, superclass, class, subclass, infraclass, order, superfamily, family, genus, species, and subspecies or variety.

Another change concerned the kinds of information that scientists use to classify organisms. The earliest naturalists used obvious physical features, such as the differences between ducks and turtles, to divide organisms into groups. By the time of Ray and Linnaeus, naturalists could study specimens in more detail. Aided by new tools such as the microscope, they explored the inner structures of plants and animals. For a long time after Linnaeus, classification was based mainly on details of anatomy, or physical structure, although scientists also looked at how an organism reproduced and how and where it lived.

Today, biologists can peer more deeply into an organism's inner workings than Aristotle or Linnaeus ever dreamed possible. They can look inside its individual cells and study the arrangement of DNA that makes up its genetic blueprint. Genetic information is key to modern classification because DNA is more than an organism's blueprint—it also reveals how closely the organism is related to other species and how long ago those species separated during the process of evolution.

In recent years, many biologists have pointed out that the Linnaean system is a patchwork of old and new ideas. It doesn't clearly reflect the latest knowledge about the evolutionary links among organisms both living and extinct. Some scientists now call for a new approach to taxonomy, one that is based entirely on evolutionary relationships. One of the most useful new approaches is called phylogenetics, the study of organisms' evolutionary histories. Using a set of organizing steps called cladistics, scientists group together all organisms that are descended from the same ancestor. The result is branching, treelike diagrams called cladograms. These cladograms show the order in which groups of plants or animals split off from their shared ancestors.

Although none of the proposed new systems of classifying living things has been accepted by all scientists, the move toward a phylogenetic approach is under way. Most experts recognize the importance of cladistics while still using the two main features of Linnaean taxonomy: the hierarchy of categories and the two-part species name. Still, scientists may disagree about the proper term for a category, or about how to classify a particular

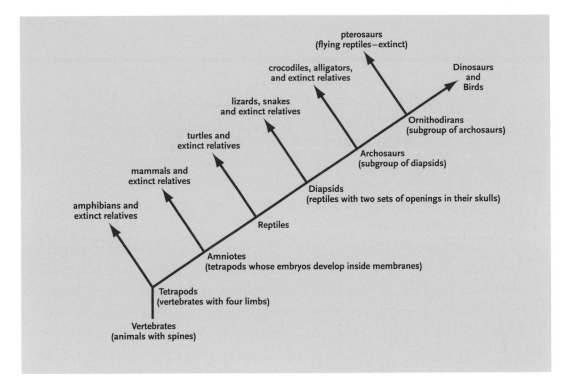

Cladograms illustrate phylogenetics, which is the study of how living things are related through evolution. A cladogram is a diagram of clades. Each clade is a group that includes an ancestor and all of its descendants. On this cladogram, all of the animals listed are descended from tetrapods. Together, they form the tetrapod clade. Smaller clades are nested within it. For example, the archosaur clade includes archosaurs and all of their descendants—crocodiles and their relatives, pterosaurs, dinosaurs, and birds.

plant or animal. Because scientists create and use classifications for many different purposes, there is no single "right" way to classify organisms.

Even at the highest level of classification, scientists take different approaches to taxonomy. A few of them still divide all life into two kingdoms, plants and animals. At the other extreme are scientists who divide life into thirteen or more kingdoms. Some now group the kingdoms into larger categories called domains or superkingdoms. Most scientists, though, use classification systems with five to seven kingdoms: plants, animals, fungi, and several kingdoms of microscopic organisms such as bacteria, amoebas, and algae.

An Example of Taxonomy:
The Common Barn Owl

Barn owls got their name because they often live around farms. One species of barn owl has the scientific name *Tyto alba*. Nonscientists call it the common barn owl.

   This bird usually measures about 15 inches (38 centimeters) in length. The common barn owl's most distinctive features are its heart-shaped white face, long legs, and golden-brown plumage. It hunts by night, locating prey with its extremely keen hearing. *Tyto alba* can live in forests, grasslands, and agricultural areas, and other environments. It can feed on birds, amphibians, lizards, and even insects in addition to its favorite prey, small rodents. Many ornithologists say that the uncommonly adaptable common barn owl is one of the world's most widespread bird species. Here is its scientific classification:

Kingdom	Animalia (animals)
Phylum	Chordata (with spinal cords)
Subphylum	Vertebrata (with segmented spines)
Superclass	Tetrapoda (amphibians, reptiles, birds, and mammals)
Class	Aves (birds)
Subclass	Neornithes (all living birds)
Superorder	Neognathae (all birds except tinamous, emus, ostriches, and their relatives)
Order	Strigiformes (owls)
Family	Tytonidae (barn owls)
Genus	*Tyto* (all barn owls except bay owls)
Species	*alba* (the common barn owl)

The classification of living things is always changing, as scientists learn more about the connections among organisms. Today, taxonomists are taking a new look at the bird class. They are considering new approaches to classifying living birds based on DNA studies, while fossil discoveries are casting more light on the link between dinosaurs and birds. At the same time, ornithologists, the scientists who study birds, are learning more about these feathered creatures, how they live, and the challenges they face in a changing world.

Scientists classify living things in arrangements like this family tree of the animal

ANIMAL

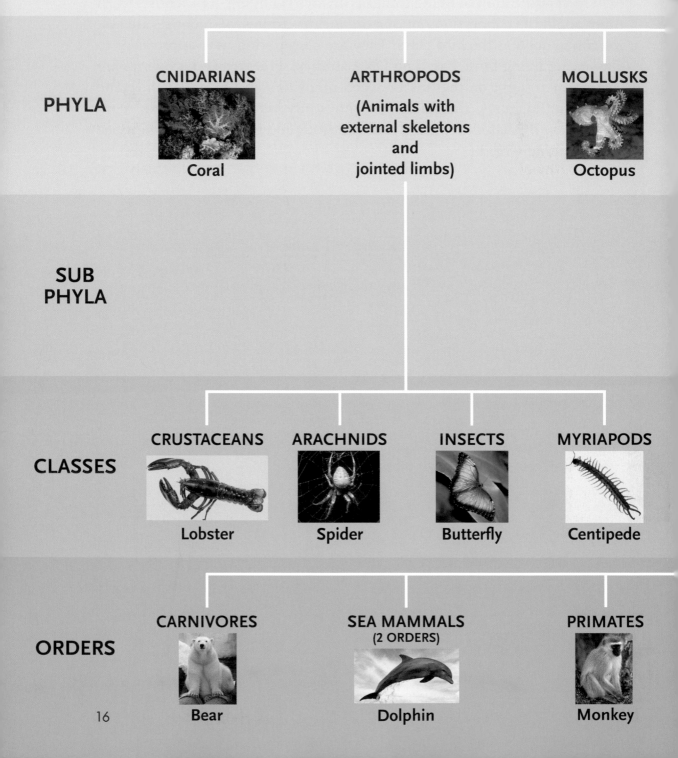

PHYLA

CNIDARIANS

Coral

ARTHROPODS
(Animals with
external skeletons
and
jointed limbs)

MOLLUSKS

Octopus

**SUB
PHYLA**

CLASSES

CRUSTACEANS

Lobster

ARACHNIDS

Spider

INSECTS

Butterfly

MYRIAPODS

Centipede

ORDERS

CARNIVORES

Bear

SEA MAMMALS
(2 ORDERS)

Dolphin

PRIMATES

Monkey

kingdom to highlight the connections and the differences among the many forms of life.

KINGDOM

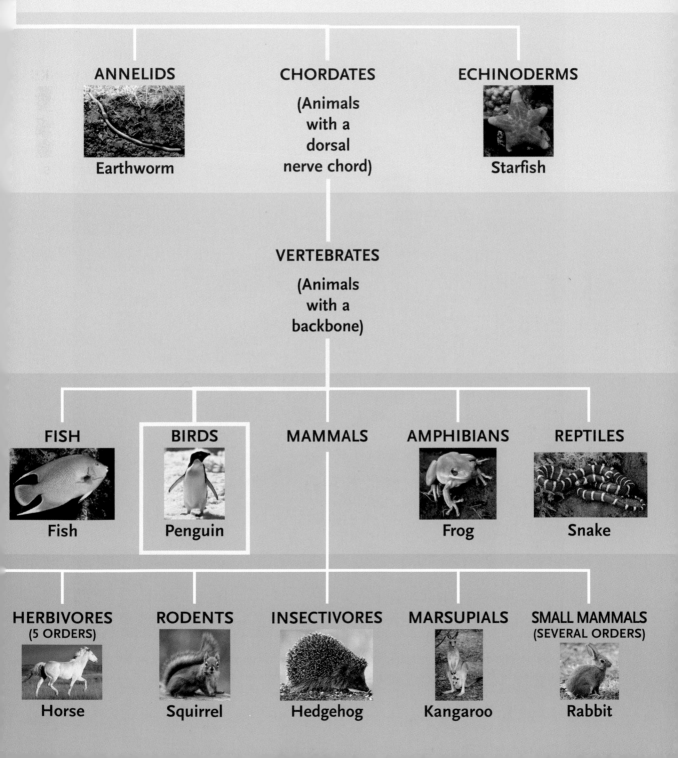

ANNELIDS

Earthworm

CHORDATES

(Animals with a dorsal nerve chord)

ECHINODERMS

Starfish

VERTEBRATES

(Animals with a backbone)

FISH

Fish

BIRDS

Penguin

MAMMALS

AMPHIBIANS

Frog

REPTILES

Snake

HERBIVORES
(5 ORDERS)

Horse

RODENTS

Squirrel

INSECTIVORES

Hedgehog

MARSUPIALS

Kangaroo

SMALL MAMMALS
(SEVERAL ORDERS)

Rabbit

Found in Wyoming, a 10-inch-tall fossil bird is 34 to 55 million years old. Fossils such as this have cast considerable light on the origins of birds, but much remains to be learned.

Avian Origins

One of the most important fossil discoveries in scientific history started with a stone feather. In 1861, workmen at a stone quarry in Solnhofen, Germany, found something unexpected on the surface of a freshly cut block of stone in the quarry. It was the impression of a feather, perfectly preserved in the stone.

People did not get excited just because a fossil feather had been found—such things had been found before. It was the *age* of this particular fossil that caused amazement. Geology, the study of the earth, was a fairly new science, but already it was known that the rock formations in the Solnhofen quarry dated from a time in the distant past called the late Jurassic period. This meant that the fossil feather was about 150 million years old. No one had dreamed that birds, the only animals with feathers, existed that long ago.

Hermann von Meyer, a German paleontologist, decided to investigate Solnhofen. Before long, he had unearthed the complete fossil of the feathered creature, which was about the size of a crow. The fossil, named *Archaeopteryx lithographica,* immediately stirred up controversy. For some people, the controversy continues to this day.

What made *Archaeopteryx* a subject of debate? It was a transitional fossil, one that showed a transition, or shift, from one kind of animal to another. *Archaeopteryx* had the teeth, bony tail, and claws of a reptile, but it also had the wings, feathers, and wishbone of a bird. Two years earlier, English naturalist Charles Darwin had predicted that people would one day find transitional fossils.

Darwin's book *On the Origin of Species* had given the world a revolutionary idea. He called it "descent with modification." Today we call Darwin's idea evolution. It is the pattern of change from one species to the next that takes place over time, as mutations in the genetic makeup of existing species gradually give rise to new, separate species. Transitional fossils, or "intermediate forms," as Darwin called them, would combine features of both old and new life forms. *Archaeopteryx*, somewhere between a reptile and a bird, was just such a fossil, and Darwin immediately saw its importance. "The fossil bird," he declared, "is a grand case for me."

That was just the problem. People who did not want to accept Darwin's idea were slow to recognize *Archaeopteryx* as a transitional fossil because that would support the idea of evolution. Richard Owen, a leading scientist of the time who was opposed to Darwin, called *Archaeopteryx* a deformed bird. That argument fell apart when other *Archaeopteryx* fossils came out of Solnhofen. Other people claimed that the fossils were fakes, cooked up to defend evolutionary biology. As recently as the 1980s, several British astronomers brought up that argument, calling *Archaeopteryx* a hoax. But the fossils have been repeatedly and thoroughly examined, and they are not fakes. Today all serious, well-qualified biologists know that *Archaeopteryx* is an authentic transitional fossil.

Yet scientists do not agree on what *Archaeopteryx* means. Most authorities regard it as the oldest known bird. A few, though, argue that *Archaeopteryx* is really a birdlike reptile, one among many such ancient animals. Experts are also uncertain about whether *Archaeopteryx* could fly. Some think that the structure of its heavy skeleton rules out true flight. Recent studies, though, suggest that *Archaeopteryx* probably could fly, but

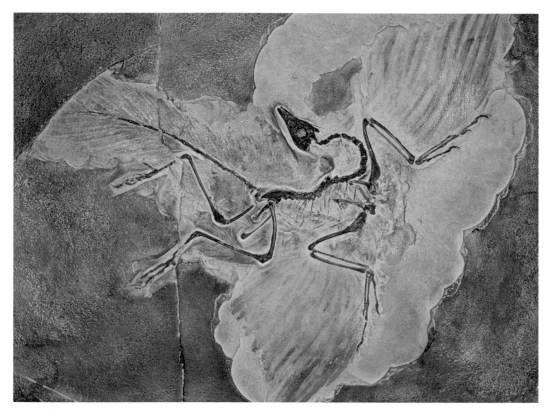

One of the most famous—and controversial—fossils ever discovered is *Archaeopteryx lithographica*, the remains of a creature midway between a reptile and a bird.

not well. It might have been better at gliding down from trees, or leaping long distances with help from its flapping wings, than powering itself through the air.

Archaeopteryx has lost its special place as the only transitional fossil between reptiles and birds. Today, the scientists who study the origins and development of birds can examine fossils of many transitional creatures, and they are finding new ones all the time. Any day, a major fossil find could dramatically change scientists' thinking about the origin of birds. For now, however, a majority of experts agree that birds evolved from dinosaurs.

DINOSAURS AND BIRDS

Dinosaurs were an enormously varied, long-lasting group of reptiles. The oldest known dinosaur fossils date from the middle of the Triassic period, about 230 million years ago. Over millions of years, some kinds of dinosaurs died out, while new kinds evolved. Around 65 million years ago, however, all of the remaining species of dinosaurs became extinct. Until recently, people thought that the closest living relatives of the dinosaurs were the reptiles: turtles, crocodiles, lizards, and snakes.

As early as the sixteenth century, some anatomists—scientists who study the physical structure of animals—had noticed many similarities between birds and reptiles. The scales on birds' legs are a lot like lizards' and snakes' scales, for example. Another similarity is that both birds and reptiles lay eggs.

In the late nineteenth century, after Darwin showed that evolution links together different kinds of life-forms, Darwin's friend and fellow scientist Thomas Henry Huxley pointed out the strong resemblance between living birds and certain dinosaur fossils. Huxley hinted at the possibility that birds might be related to, or descended from, dinosaurs. Few scientists took this idea seriously. Most of them thought that birds had evolved from some other reptile ancestor. Dinosaurs, they believed, had left no descendants.

The dinosaur-bird connection came back to life in the 1970s, largely through the work of an American paleontologist named John H. Ostrom. In 1969 Ostrom published a study of a fossil dinosaur that he had discovered in Montana. Ostrom suggested that this dinosaur, called *Deinonychus*, might have been warm-blooded. Up to that point, scientists had been sure that the dinosaurs, like lizards and other living reptiles, were cold-blooded. Ostrom made a case that some of the two-legged dinosaurs could have been warm-blooded and fast-moving. Their movements and ways of life, he argued, made them seem more like modern birds than like lizards. In 1973 Ostrom presented the idea that a group of dinosaurs called theropods were the ancestors of birds.

Ostrom's ideas about dinosaurs and birds were revolutionary. Science did not accept his thinking at first. Not until many other researchers had taken a new look at dinosaur fossils did Ostrom's ideas start to gain support in the scientific community. Then, in the 1990s, a series of sensational fossil discoveries strengthened the dinosaur-bird connection. Scientists found new transitional species of birdlike dinosaurs and dinosaurlike birds. These fossils suggest that the link between dinosaurs and birds is real. Not all scientists agree. Some think that birds evolved from a different group of reptiles, but the evidence for these claims is not as strong as the evidence for a dinosaur origin. Even the experts who agree that birds evolved from dinosaurs, however, do not yet understand all the details.

Avian ancestors almost certainly came from the large category of dinosaurs known as theropods. These were carnivorous dinosaurs that ran upright on two legs. One group of theropods, known as the coelurosaurs, developed a coating of hollow, threadlike tubes or downy fibers. Biologists call these coatings "protofeathers," which means "beginning of feathers." *Sinosauropteryx*, the first feathered dinosaur to be discovered, belongs to this group.

Sinosauropteryx fossils from China show that featherlike structures existed on some ancient creatures that were not birds.

One group of coelurosaurs evolved into the tyrannosaurs, a category that included *Tyrannosaurus rex* and many other dinosaurs. Another group of coelurosaurs, the maniraptorans, led to the ancestors of birds. There were three main categories of maniraptorans: troodontids, dromaeosaurs (including the velociraptors, fast-moving, predatory dinosaurs that may have hunted in packs), and avialans. All three categories contained winged, feathered, birdlike creatures. Some paleontologists think that modern birds are descended from troodontids or dromaeosaurs. Others pinpoint the origins of today's birds within the avialans, a group that included *Archaeopteryx* and other early birds whose feathers were just like the feathers of modern birds.

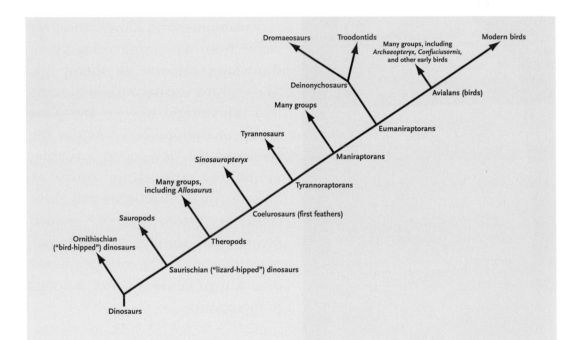

This cladogram illustrates some of the current ideas about the evolution of birds. Modern birds are descended from the avialans, which also gave rise to *Archaeopteryx* and other early birds. (Some experts think that modern birds may have descended from birdlike dromaeosaurs or troodontids.) In the phylogenetic view, birds are part of the dinosaur clade.

Mei long, the first fossil ever found of a sleeping dinosaur, may be a clue to the ancient origins of some modern bird behavior. This small birdlike troodontid slept in a position similar to that of a sleeping duck.

These early birds shared a number of physical features with some of the coelurosaurs, especially with the maniraptorans. Both the birds and the dinosaurs stood upright, on two legs, supported by feet that had three main toes. Their legs moved forward and back when they walked, not out to the sides like the legs of crocodiles and lizards. The eggshells and teeth of the birds were also very similar to those of the dinosaurs.

Their skeletons had points of similarity, too. In both groups, the two parts of the collarbone fused together to form a single structure called the furcula, or wishbone. Another similarity involves pneumaticity, which means air-filled spaces within the bones. Most animals have fairly solid bones with a material called marrow filling their centers. Birds, however, have thin-walled, hollow bones, and so did some dinosaurs. In birds, these bones contain sacs that fill with air because they are connected to the lungs.

There is evidence that dinosaurs also had air sacs in their bones. Scientists are not sure why pneumatic—or air-filled— bones evolved. One idea is that air-filled bones allowed animals to evolve toward larger sizes. Such bones are lighter than marrow-filled bones, so they take less energy to maintain and move. Size and pneumaticity do seem to go together. The highest degree of pneumaticity in dinosaur bones is found in the largest theropods, including the tyrannosaurs. The same is true of flying birds today. Large birds, such as vultures and pelicans, have pneumatic bones throughout most of their skeletons. Smaller birds, such as songbirds, have pneumatic bones only near their lungs.

Hollow, air-filled bones offer a big energy savings when animals fly, because lighter bones are easier to lift and propel with muscle power. Pneumatic bones evolved before birds and their ancestors took to the air, but they were an evolutionary advantage that contributed to flight.

Birds were not the only vertebrates that developed the ability to fly. The pterosaurs were ancient flying reptiles that did not belong to the dinosaur category; they became extinct and left no descendants in the modern world. Flight developed among the mammals, too—in bats. Flight is a good example of what biologists call convergent evolution. This means that separate evolutionary paths converge, or come to the same place. In the case of pterosaurs, birds, and bats, three different lines of evolution led to flight.

Flight is useful for many things—escaping from predators, catching fast-moving prey, reaching new sources of food or shelter. But how did animals move from climbing, running, and walking to flying? There are two contrasting theories about the origins of flight. The "trees down" theory says that flight started with animals gliding downward from tree branches, as flying squirrels do today. Flaps of skin on their forelimbs gradually evolved into wings. In the "ground up" theory, flight began with animals leaping off the ground. Flaps of skin on their forelimbs helped them sail higher and farther, and these gradually evolved into wings.

Scientists will probably never know which theory is correct. Although fossils show that forelimbs evolved into wings, fossils cannot tell us how the animals used those forelimbs and wings. Experts do know, however, that the flight of modern birds depends on a number of evolutionary adaptations. Among these are wristbones that swivel to allow a rotating wingstroke, and a breastbone with a thick ridge called a keel that anchors the strong chest muscles birds need to move their wings. These and other features that support flight appeared over time in dinosaurs and ancient birds.

Confuciusornis, another creature known from Chinese fossils, was about the size of a modern pigeon, with a long, feathered tail. One of the most ancient birds known, it lived more than 120 million years ago.

ANCIENT BIRDS

A fossil found in Texas in 1984 could have rewritten the story of bird evolution. The fossil was about 220 million years old. Its discoverer named it *Protoavis*, "beginning of birds," and declared that it was the oldest fossil bird ever found—70 million years or more older than *Archaeopteryx*.

Many experts disagreed. *Protoavis* was not a complete fossil, or even a mostly complete one. It was assembled from separate pieces that, most paleontologists think, could well belong to other animals, not birds. As a result, *Protoavis* is not generally regarded as part of the story of bird evolution. *Archaeopteryx* remains the oldest known bird. Another ancient bird, *Confuciusornis*, lived almost as long ago as *Archaeopteryx*. Like *Archaeopteryx*, *Confuciusornis* had claws on its wings, but unlike *Archaeopteryx*, it did not have teeth.

The flightless dodo is now as extinct as *Archaeopteryx*, but it lived on islands in the Indian Ocean until the seventeenth century. The dodo was wiped out by humans and the pigs and dogs they brought to the islands.

Neither *Archaeopteryx* nor *Confuciusornis* is known to be a direct ancestor of modern birds. The ancient world had many bird lineages, or lines of descent. The interrelationships among these lineages are mysterious, and it will take time and study—and more fossil finds—to sort them out. But although paleontologists do not yet know exactly how modern birds are connected to ancient birds, they have begun to fill in the picture.

During the Cretaceous period, from 65 to 144 million years ago, many new groups of birds appeared. One well-studied group is the hesperornithiformes. The birds in this group had teeth, and most of them had small wings. They probably could not fly, but paleontologists think that they could have been good swimmers who moved themselves through the water by paddling their powerful feet. The ichthyornithiformes were another group of toothed birds, but they were fliers. These birds, along with other now-extinct varieties, lived alongside members of some modern bird groups, such as loons, geese, ducks, chickens, albatrosses, and gulls. All of these groups of modern birds, and possibly a few others, had evolved into existence by the end of the Cretaceous period.

Like the dinosaurs, many ancient lineages of birds became extinct around 65 million years ago. Those that survived continued to evolve into a great variety of new forms. The phororhachids were large, flightless carnivores that could run fast and snatch their prey with huge beaks and claws. These birds ranged from South America to Florida, and some of them were 10 feet (3 m) tall. Phororhachids were the main South American predators for millions of years. The diatrymids, who lived in North America and Europe, were similar to the phororhachids. Both groups probably resembled modern ratites, a category of large running birds that includes ostriches. Neither the phororhachids nor the diatrymids were the ancestors of the ratites, however. They died out without leaving any descendants in the modern world.

By about 35 million years ago, most of the modern bird groups had evolved. They had spread across the world to occupy a wide range of habitats. Among them were parrots, owls, crows, penguins, songbirds, and other close relatives of the birds that we know today.

China's Fantastic Feathered Fossils

Liaoning Province in northeastern China, a day's drive from the capital, is a region of farms and factories. About 130 million years ago, though, it was a warm landscape of lakes and forests, dotted with smoldering volcanoes. Occasionally one of those volcanoes erupted. When this happened, thick, fine ash blanketed the land and sank into the lakes, burying all kinds of creatures and plants.

Over millions of years, the buried plants and animals slowly turned to stone. They became fossils—some of the most detailed, finely preserved fossils that modern scientists have ever found. Conditions in the layers of ash and sand at the bottom of Liaoning's ancient ponds and lakes were perfect for preserving soft tissues, the non-bony body parts of animals that do not appear in most fossils. Some fossils from Liaoning show insect wings, feathers, the patterns of spots and stripes on preserved skin, and even the stomach contents of animals that died after eating.

Local people have been finding fossils in Liaoning for centuries. The Chinese government now controls fossil collecting, but many discoveries are still made by farmers, some of whom work with teams of visiting scientists. Since the early 1990s, Liaoning's fossil beds have offered up a stream of exciting discoveries. The most famous are the feathered dinosaurs and early birds. Dinosaur fossils with evidence of wings, feathers, and other birdlike features provide strong evidence of the connection between dinosaurs and birds.

Sinosauropteryx is one of the most important fossils found at Liaoning. It is clearly feathered, yet it is a dinosaur, not a bird. Discovered in 1996, it was the first proof of feathered dinosaurs. Other signficant finds include *Dilong paradoxus,* a tyannosaur (and smaller cousin of the mighty *T. rex*) covered with a thin coat of fibers or fuzz that may have been an early form of feathers; *Microraptor gui,* a birdlike dinosaur with feathers very similar to those of modern birds; and *Confuciusornis sanctus,* an ancient bird that lived alongside the dinosaurs and had long tail feathers.

In 2004, Liaoning yielded another remarkable fossil: *Mei long,* a birdlike member of the troodontid group of dinosaurs. *Mei long* was smaller than a modern chicken, with a long, thin tail and short, winglike forelimbs. The first dinosaur fossil ever found in a sleeping position, was buried in ash while it slept, with its legs folded under it, its long, flexible neck curved back across its body, and its head tucked beneath its forelimb. This sleeping position is exactly like that used today by ducks and other birds. The scientists who found *Mei long,* Xu Xing and Mark Norell, think that their little sleeping dinosaur means that some kinds of bird behavior could have originated in small dinosaurs, before true birds split off from the dinosaur family.

Many questions remain about the evolution of feathers, flight, and birds. A Liaoning farmer digging in his field, or a paleontologist excavating one of the region's ancient lake bottoms, may make the next big discovery that will answer some of those questions.

Hovering to feed on flower nectar, a broad-billed hummingbird uses rapid, rotating wingbeats to stay in one place—a type of bird flight that scientists once thought impossible.

The Orders of Modern Birds

How many species of birds live in the world today? The answer depends on which scientist you ask. Most ornithologists place the total number of living bird species somewhere between 9,000 and 10,000, with many of the experts favoring figures closer to 10,000. The species are grouped into approximately two thousand genera, and the genera are gathered into between 180 and 200 families. Finally, the families fall into two or three dozen orders in the subclass Neornithes, which includes all modern birds. The class Aves, or birds, contains Neornithes and other subclasses that are now extinct.

TURBULENT TAXONOMY

Bird taxonomy is in the middle of an upheaval. The traditional list of orders is being revised on the basis of DNA studies, but the process is slow and uncertain because the studies' results are not always clear. They must be confirmed and debated by the scientific community. In the meantime, the taxonomy of the birds is like an unfinished construction project, with the plan constantly changing.

Several different schemes for classifying birds are now in use. Most of them start by dividing modern birds into two large categories based on differences in the shape of the bony palate, the hard plate in the roof of the mouth. These two categories are the superorders Paleognathae ("old jaws") and Neognathae ("new jaws"). The Neognathae are then subdivided into two infraorders, the Galloanserae and the Neoaves.

The superorder Paleognathae contains two orders and half a dozen or so families of birds. So does the infraorder Galloanersae, one of the two infraorders of the Neognathae. The other infraorder of Neognathae, called the Neoaves or "new birds," contains most of the bird orders, families, and species in the world today. Together, the orders of all three categories show a vast variety of avian physical adaptations, habitats, and ways of life.

" O L D   J A W S "

The superorder Paleognathae contains two orders. One order, the Tinamiformes, has a single family—the shy, fast-running, ground-dwelling South American birds called tinamous. Tinamous can fly, but they usually do so only for short distances. Some researchers consider tinamous to be the closest of all living birds to the ancestral bird lineage.

The other order of paleognath birds is the Struthioniformes, also called the ratites. Unlike tinamous, ratites are flightless. Scientists think that they evolved from flying ancestors and later lost the ability to fly. The smallest family of ratites, the kiwis of New Zealand, are short-legged birds that live in burrows and forage on the forest floor by night. The remaining ratite families are all diurnal, or active by day. These large, shaggy-feathered, long-legged birds are fast runners. They are the African ostrich, the rheas of South America, the emus of Australia, and the cassowaries of Australia and New Guinea.

One ratite, *Struthio camelus*, or the ostrich, is the largest living bird. It can reach heights of 9 feet (2.7 m) and weights of 300 pounds (136 kilograms).

The yellow-legged tinamou, shown in the Atlantic rain forest of eastern Brazil, is one of several dozen species of these ground-nesting birds found in Central and South America.

Two groups of ratites that became extinct within the past few centuries were even larger. The moas of New Zealand could weigh as much as 500 pounds (227 kg) and reach heights of up to 10 feet (3 m) when their necks were stretched upward. The elephant birds of the African island of Madagascar were shorter but much more massive. The biggest species weighed 1,000 pounds (454 kg). Its enormous egg had a volume of about 2 gallons (7.6 liters).

GAME BIRDS AND WATERFOWL

Within the superorder Neognathae, game birds and waterfowl are set apart from other birds and placed in the infraorder Galloanserae. Game birds belong to the order Galliformes, which includes chickens and their

The bare-faced currasow lives in the forests of Bolivia and Brazil. It feeds on the ground by day and roosts on tree branches by night to evade predators such as jaguars.

relatives. They are called game birds because they are widely hunted for food. Pheasants (including peacocks), quail, turkeys, and grouse are all game birds. So are the guinea fowl of Africa, the megapodes of Australia and the South Pacific, and the guans, chachalacas, and currasows of South America. Most game birds live on the ground, although a few are arboreal, or tree-dwelling. They typically fly only for short distances.

The order Anseriformes contains the waterfowl. These are ducks, geese, swans, and screamers, a gooselike family of loud-calling birds that lives in South American wetlands. As the name suggests, waterfowl live near water: rivers, lakes, marshes, ponds, and seacoasts. They are strong swimmers. Most of them are also excellent fliers and can travel long distances by air.

INFRAORDER NEOAVES

The second subdivision of the Neognathae is the infraorder Neoaves. This category includes several dozen orders of birds, from penguins to hummingbirds.

Penguins

Penguins belong to the order Sphenisciformes, which contains one family and half a dozen genera. Penguins have large keels on their breastbones that support enough muscle to move their wings, but they cannot fly. Their wings have evolved into strong, flat flippers that help make the birds

Emperor penguins "fly" toward the surface after diving for fish in the icy waters off Antarctica.

outstanding swimmers and divers. In a way, penguins fly underwater, steering with their webbed feet. They feed on fish, shrimp, and krill in the chilly seas of the Southern Hemisphere, including the Antarctic Ocean. Penguins' feathers are well adapted to this cold-water way of life. Each of the short feathers has fluffy down at its base. This down insulates the penguin by trapping air that holds body heat, keeping the bird warm. The tips of the feathers are stiff, scaly, and oily. They form a sleek protective coat that keeps the down dry.

Divers

The order Gaviiformes contains one family, the divers of northern North America and Eurasia. These birds are also called loons for their loud cries,

The chick of a common loon hitches a ride on its protective parent's back.

which some people think sound like crazy laughter or sorrowful wailing. Another family of swimming and diving birds, the grebes, forms the order Podicipediformes. Both divers and grebes spend most of their time hunting for freshwater fish, worms, and other aquatic food. They nest near ponds and lakes. When the chicks hatch, they ride around on the backs of their swimming parents for protection from predators such as turtles and large fish.

Tube-nosed Seabirds

Four families of tube-nosed seabirds—the albatrosses, shearwaters, petrels, and fulmars— make up the order Procellariiformes. These birds range far out over the open ocean, feeding on fish and squid. A few of them are known to eat other birds. Giant fulmars, for example, snatch up and devour penguins. All of the birds in this order can drink seawater, which is too salty for most animals. The Procellariiformes have a special gland at the base of their bill that removes the excess salt from the water. The salt dribbles out through their nostrils, which take the form of tubes on the tops or sides of their bills.

Flamingoes

A specialized bill is also a feature of the flamingoes, members of the only family in the order Phoenicopteriformes. Flamingoes feed on tiny creatures such as brine shrimp that live in the shallow waters of lakes and lagoons in Africa, South America, the Caribbean islands, the Mediterranean region, and southern Asia. The flamingo's bill is bent sharply downward in the middle, unlike that of any other bird. The flamingo's way of feeding is also unique. It eats with its head upside down, resting its upper bill on the mud. Its muscular tongue sucks water into the mouth. The water strains out through fine plates on the edge of the bill, leaving food matter behind in the flamingo's mouth.

Pelicans and Relatives

The Pelecaniformes are an order of six families of pelicans, tropicbirds, boobies and gannets, anhingas, cormorants, and frigate birds. All are fish-eaters who live near water. Some of them, such as tropicbirds and brown pelicans, dive on their prey from great heights. Others, such as cormorants, boobies, and gannets, plunge from the air but also chase their prey underwater. White pelicans feed cooperatively. They gather in a flock on the water and then flap their wings and beat their feet to drive fish into shallow water, where it is easier to catch them. Frigate birds have a method of feeding called kleptoparasitism, or piracy. A frigate bird waits until a gull or other seabird has caught a fish. It then chases and harasses the bird until it drops or vomits the prey, which the frigate bird then catches in midair. Most birds in the order Pelecaniformes have long bills, and their bills or throats contain pouches that can expand to hold food. The largest pouch, the pelican's, holds three times as much food as the bird's stomach does.

A brown pelican engulfs a fish. The catch will be stored in the bird's gular pouch, the large throat sac attached to its bill. Pelicans can catch fish by either plunge-diving or by skimming the surface with open bills.

Shorebirds

The members of the order Charadriiformes are also found near water. This order has sixteen to eighteen families. These include gulls, terns, skuas, kittiwakes, oystercatchers, sandpipers, auks, puffins, curlews, skimmers, stilts, plovers, and their relatives. Some feed in fresh water, some in salt water, and some in both. Some nest on beaches, while others lay their eggs on cliffs and sea rocks. Among the birds of this order are waders, swimmers, and divers. One group, the jacanas of the tropics, travel by picking their way across the tops of floating water plants, such as lily pads.

The Atlantic puffin is a diving bird of the cold northern waters.

Waders

The Ciconiiformes are the order of herons, storks, ibises, egrets, and other long-legged (and sometimes long-necked) wading birds. Many of these birds feed in water, eating mostly fish and frogs. Storks and some egrets, however, feed mostly on land. Their diet includes insects, reptiles, and even small mammals such as mice. Most birds in this order have

In the United States, the graceful white birds known as cattle egrets are seen perched atop cows. This egret in the African nation of Tanzania rides a hippopotamus. As the hippo plows through water lettuce, the bird can snatch up tiny fish or bugs disturbed by the hippo's passage.

long, strong, pointed bills for stabbing, but a few have distinctive bill shapes. Ibises use their downward-curving bills to probe into mud and soil. Spoonbills have flat, spoon-shaped bills for scooping up mud in search of food. The African shoebill or whale-headed stork, *Balaeniceps rex,* uses its massive hooked bill to seize prey as large as a 4-foot-long (1.2-meter-long) lungfish.

Cranes and Relatives

Like storks and herons, cranes are long-legged and long-necked, but they belong to a different order, the Gruiformes. The dozen or so families in this diverse order include cranes, large birds that fly well and inhabit open plains and swamps, as well as smaller, shy birds such as rails, which fly weakly or not at all and live in reedy marshes. Among the other families are limpkins, crakes, coots, gallinules, and bustards. Some little-known

The purple gallinule is found from the southern United States south to Argentina.

members of this order are the roatelos, fast-running birds that flock in the forests and brushlands of Madagascar, and *Rhynochetos jubatus*, the kagu, which is a crested, nocturnal, nearly flightless bird found only on the Pacific island of New Caledonia.

Birds of prey

The Falconiformes are another diverse group. This order has four or five families, dozens of genera, and more than three hundred species of eagles, hawks, ospreys, vultures, and falcons worldwide. With sharp, hooked beaks, powerful legs, long claws on their feet, and extremely keen eyesight, these birds of prey are formidable hunters. Secretary birds walk in search of their prey, usually lizards and snakes, but the others hunt while in flight. Ospreys snatch fish out of the water. Hawks and eagles swoop from above to catch prey on the ground. Falcons dive at smaller birds in midair. The fastest bird, *Falco peregrinus* or the peregrine falcon, can reach bursts of up to

Although it flies well and nests in trees, the secretary bird of Africa is a ground-hunting carnivore that stalks the grasslands in search of live prey. It may be as much as 46 inches (66 cm) tall.

200 miles per hour (320 kilometers per hour) when diving. Vultures and condors feed mostly on the carcasses of dead animals, and other birds of prey also scavenge dead carrion from time to time. The majestic bald eagle, for example, will eat dead salmon.

Owls

One group of birds of prey, the owls, have their own order, called the Strigiformes. Unlike other birds, whose eyes are set on the sides of narrow, wedge-shaped heads, owls have forward-facing eyes set in a flat, disk-shaped face. This gives them a broader range of binocular, or two-eyed, vision than most birds. Binocular vision is good for judging how far away things are. Owls cannot see far around to each side the way birds with side-facing eyes can do, but owls can still get a side view without turning their bodies to look. They can rotate their heads so far around that they almost seem to have their heads on backward.

Other birds of prey are diurnal, but owls are nocturnal. They are adapted to hunting at night for their favorite food, small mammals such as mice and voles. Owls' large eyes gather a lot of light, so they see well in dim conditions. Their hearing is very good, and their ears have an unusual feature. The ear canal on one side of an owl's head is higher than the ear canal on the other side. A sound reaches the two ears at slightly different times, and this tiny difference lets the bird pinpoint the sound's location. Even in total darkness an owl can plunge directly onto a mouse rustling through the grass.

Nightbirds

The order Caprimulgiformes includes the nightjars, poorwills, frogmouths, oilbirds, and potoos. These birds are either nocturnal or crepuscular, active at dusk. By day they sleep in trees, on the ground, or, in the case of the oilbirds, in caves. All nightbirds have cryptic coloration, which means that the colors and patterns of their feathers help them blend into their backgrounds. It is hard for a birdwatcher—or a predator—to spot these birds when they are well camouflaged and perfectly still.

Mousebirds

The order Coliiformes contains one family with half a dozen species of colis, also known as mousebirds. These small African birds move about in flocks of twenty or so, chirping and scampering

Where does the branch end and the bird begin? Cryptic coloration helps a common potoo blend into its perch, a broken branch.

across the ground like mice. With drab gray or brown plumage, all mousebirds are "mousy," but they have bright red feet. These feet are very flexible, allowing the birds to climb nimbly in trees and shrubs. Mousebirds are herbivorous, devouring seeds, fruit, berries, and buds.

Trogons

Another order that contains about half a dozen species is Trogoniformes, the trogons. Found in tropical areas of the Americas, Africa, and Asia, these are long-tailed, brightly colored birds that eat fruit, insects, snails, and frogs. They favor forest habitats because they make their nests in hollow stumps or holes they peck in trees. One trogon, *Pharomachrus mocinno*, the resplendent quetzal, has especially brilliant, iridescent green and red coloring and long tail feathers. It was once a sacred bird to the Maya people of Central America, and today it is the national bird of Guatemala.

The quetzal is now a protected species in Mexico, Guatemala, Costa Rica, and Panama. Illegal captures continue, but a network of forest preserves in Costa Rica offers refuge for these birds, which live in cool, dense tropical mountain forest and eat fruit and small prey.

Kingfishers are often spotted in trees that overhang streams and rivers. They dive into the water for prey and return to their perches to devour it.

Kingfishers and Relatives

With several hundred species in ten or so families, the order Coraciiformes is found on every continent except Antarctica. This order contains the king-fishers (including the Australian kookaburra) and a number of related birds, such as rollers, motmots, hoopoes, and bee-eaters. All of them are carnivores. The kingfishers plunge into streams for fish, and the bee-eaters catch bees in midflight. The hornbills, the largest birds in the order, stalk on the ground searching for frogs, lizards, and insects. Some members of this order also eat fruits and berries.

Pigeons and Doves

The order Columbiformes contains the family of pigeons and doves (there is no scientific difference between the two terms, which may refer to the same birds). These plump, soft-voiced birds have short legs, necks, and bills. *Columba livia,* the rock dove or rock pigeon, has evolved in-to a bird that is a familiar sight in many cities of the world: the common pigeon. Certain kinds of pigeons are easily domesticated. Pigeon-breeding has long been a popular pastime in some parts of the world. Varieties of domestic rock doves that find their way home to their roosts over long distances are called homing pigeons; they have been used for centuries to carry messages.

Closely related to the pigeons are the sandgrouse, which live in deserts and other dry, open areas of Africa and Eurasia. Sandgrouse fly to water holes to soak the feathers of their chests and bellies, then return to their nests. The water keeps their eggs from losing the moisture that the embryos inside need as they develop. Later, when the eggs have hatched, the young chicks will drink water from the parent's feathers. Some taxonomists include sandgrouse with pigeons in the order Columbiformes, while others place them in their own order, the Pteroclidiformes.

Parrots

The approximately 370 species of parrots, parakeets, cockatoos, cockatiels, macaws, lories, budgerigars and their relatives belong to the order Psittaciformes. Birds in this order vary greatly both in color and in size. The largest species is the 40-inch (102 cm) scarlet macaw, *Ara macao*, of South America's Amazon region. The smallest species is the 3.5-inch (9-cm) buff-faced pygmy parrot, *Micropsitta pusio*, which lives on the island of Papua New Guinea, north of Australia.

A hyacinth macaw uses its dextrous claw and strong beak to open a palm nut.

People have admired parrots and their kin for a long time, and some of these birds are popular as pets. Parrots are highly intelligent and, in most species, quite social. They are good at handling things with their feet, which have two forward-pointing and two backward-pointing toes that work together like a hand with an opposable thumb. (Most parrots are left-footed, although scientists do not know why.) Parrots can also manipulate objects with their heavy curved bills. Although some species in Australia and New Guinea cannot fly, most birds in the order Psittaciformes are good flyers. They spend much of their time clambering about in trees, looking for fruit.

Cuckoos and Relatives

The order Cuculiformes contains cuckoos, anis, and roadrunners. All are long-tailed birds that can run fast, either on the ground or along tree branches. Some species practice a type of parenting called nest parasitism. They lay their eggs in the nests of other birds. The other birds incubate the cuckoos' eggs. After the eggs hatch, the parent birds feed and tend the cuckoo chicks, usually at the expense of their own young— newly hatched cuckoos destroy their foster parents' eggs or chicks.

Roadrunners, native to the American Southwest, can reach speeds of up to 17 miles per hour (27 km per hour) when fleeing predators, but they spend most of their time walking in search of lizards and snakes, their usual prey.

African birds called turacos are closely related to cuckoos. Some taxonomists place them in the same order. Others give the turacos their own order, called the Musophagiformes. The same taxonomic question arises with the hoatzin, *Opisthocomus hoazin,* a crested, red-eyed South American bird that lives amid water plants and feeds on their leaves. Young hoatzins have claws on their wings to help them grip and climb on the plants, so that they do not fall into the water below; these claws disappear as the bird grows up. Hoatzins are sometimes grouped with the Cuculiformes and sometimes placed in a separate order, Opisthocomiformes.

Woodpeckers and Relatives

Woodpeckers, sapsuckers, flickers, puffbirds, barbets, and jacamars belong to the order Piciformes. Toucans, tropical birds with huge, colorful bills, are also found in this order. The Piciformes have a wide variety of feeding methods. Sapsuckers drill holes in trees and suck the sap that wells up inside the holes. Honeyguides probe beehives for bees and wax. Jacamars eat butterflies and other flying insects. Toucans eat fruit. Woodpeckers cling to trees, pecking into the bark to get insects; some species also eat seeds and acorns. Woodpeckers' toes are opposable, like those of parrots, which gives them a good grip on vertical

A toucan's large bill is lighter than it looks because it is mostly hollow. The bird uses its long, narrow tongue, which has many bristles or small spines, to move food into just the right position in its mouth so that it can tip its head back to swallow.

tree trunks. Their tail feathers are stiff, so the birds can use their tails to brace themselves against the trunks while they peck. Finally, woodpeckers have thick skulls, to withstand the impact of pounding against wood.

Hummingbirds and Swifts

More than four hundred species of hummingbirds and swifts make up the order Apodiformes. The family of swifts includes about sixty-six species. They are found worldwide, except in New Zealand and other mid-ocean islands. Swifts are gray or brown birds with short legs, tiny feet, and long, curved, pointed wings. They may appear drab, but they are some of the most acrobatic fliers in the world. Large flocks of swifts can sometimes be seen at dusk, wheeling and darting across the sky as they dine on insects caught in flight. Swifts seldom land on branches or on the ground. To rest, they

True to its name, this chimney swift has built its nest in a brick chimney. The swift's young will leave the nest before cold weather brings the chimney into use.

are more likely to cling to vertical surfaces, such as cliffs and the sides of buildings. They nest on these vertical surfaces, too, using saliva to glue slings of twigs and grass to the walls. The edible saliva of some swifts' nests is used as an ingredient in birds' nest soup, a delicacy in Asia.

A related family, the crested swifts, has just three species, found in Southeast Asia. With forked tails, crests of feathers on their foreheads, and metallic plumage, they are striking birds. Unlike swifts, the crested swifts frequently roost in trees.

More than three hundred species of hummingbirds live in the Americas, mostly in the tropics. One of them, *Mellisuga helenae*, the bee hummingbird of Cuba, is often called the world's smallest bird. It is about 2 inches (5 cm) in length. The largest bird in the family is *Patagona gigas*, the giant hummingbird of the Andes Mountains, which can reach lengths of more than 8 inches (20 cm).

Hummingbirds are known for their small size, for their long bills adapted for drinking nectar from inside flowers of many shapes and sizes, and for their brilliant, jewel-colored, iridescent feathers. They are also known for their unique flying abilities. Before European scientists began studying the birds of the Americas, they were quite sure that no bird could fly backward. The hummingbird proved them wrong. It can not only fly backward, it can move up and down or hover in one spot like a helicopter. The secret is in the hummingbird's anatomy. Hummingbirds have a shoulder joint that lets their wings swivel, or move through a wide range of angles. By whirling their wings forward, backward, up, and down, the birds can move in any direction. Moving the wings rapidly forward and back in a figure-eight motion, for example, makes the hummingbird rise straight up.

The power to hover comes from rapid wingbeats. Hummingbirds' wings typically beat so fast that they simply look like a blur. It takes a lot of muscle, and a lot of energy, to move wings that fast. A hummingbird's wing muscles usually make up a quarter to a third of its total body weight. The bird's metabolism, or body chemistry, is adapted to provide extra energy to the muscle cells. The cost is high, however. A hummingbird's heart may beat as fast as 615 beats per minute. Although humming-birds eat insects for protein, they need a lot of sugar-rich nectar to meet their energy needs. At night or when the weather turns cool, their metab-olisms slow down and they enter a state called torpor, with lower body temperatures to save energy.

Perching Birds

By far the largest bird order is the Passeriformes, or passerines, also called the perching birds. With nearly six thousand species, the passerines are the

The woodpecker finch's large feet and strong back-pointing toes—a passerine characteristic—give the bird a good grip while it uses a cactus spine to pry beetle larvae from the dead wood. Woodpecker finches were the first birds recognized as tool users.

most numerous birds in every part of the world except Antarctica. Some are carnivores, some are herbivores, and some eat both animal and plant foods.

The birds in this large and diverse order are set apart from other birds by the structure of their feet. Most modern birds have four toes. Generally, three toes point forward and one, called the hallux, points backward. On birds that spend a lot of time walking on the ground, such as ostriches and chickens, the hallux is either missing or is partway up the leg so that it does not catch on the ground. The toes of some birds are adapted to special uses. Birds of prey, for example, have powerful toes tipped with sharp claws, or

The toes and claws of birds of prey, such as this bald eagle, are specially designed to catch and hold food.

This western tanager wears the bright red-orange of the spring and summer breeding season. During winter his head and body will be a paler yellow.

talons, for seizing prey. Penguins, ducks, and other swimmers have webs of skin between their toes so that their feet can be used as paddles.

The feet of passerines are well designed for perching on branches and twigs. They have three forward-pointing toes and a backward-pointing hallux that is long and flexible enough to wrap around a perch. Their claws are generally long for the birds' size, and curved to grip branches. Passerines' leg muscles are adapted to perching, too—they tighten automatically if the bird starts to lose its hold. This lets the birds sleep on branches without falling off.

The passerines share a few other features. All of them have twelve tail feathers. All of them produce chicks that are blind, featherless, and helpless when they hatch. Young passerines need a high amount of parental care before they can leave the nest. In most species, both parents tend the young.

In spite of their shared features, passerines vary greatly in color, habits, and habitats. Some, such as wrens and creepers, are brown and inconspicuous. Others, such as scarlet tanagers and green broadbills, are brightly

"Chick-a-dee-dee" is the repeated song of the black-capped chickadee, one of the most common birds in North America. This small, sociable seed eater is a frequent visitor at many backyard feeders.

colored, while plumed passerines, such as the lyrebirds and the birds of paradise, have some of the showiest plumage in the bird world. In size, passerines range from the 4-inch (10-cm) kinglets to the 26-inch (66-cm) ravens. Their feeding habits cover a wide range, too. Sunbirds, which live in Africa and Asia, feed mostly on nectar, like hummingbirds. Dippers, the only aquatic passerines, hop and swim in fast-flowing mountain streams to catch insects and other small creatures. *Corvus corone* is not a picky eater, a fact that is suggested by its common name, carrion crow (carrion is any dead animal). It raids other birds' nest for eggs and pokes through garbage for food scraps. Crows, which are highly intelligent birds, have even learned how to use passing automobiles as nutcrackers to crush hard nuts, such as walnuts, that they cannot open with their bills.

Taxonomists divide the passerines into two suborders, the oscines and the suboscines. The difference between them lies in the syrinx, the part of the windpipe that allows birds to make sounds. Oscines have complex syrinxes. Depending upon the species, they can make a wide variety of sounds, including fluid, musical whistling or piping notes strung together in rapid sequences. This is why oscines are commonly known as songbirds. The suboscines, such as antbirds, ovenbirds, and woodcreepers, have simpler syrinxes. They cannot sing by stringing notes together. Instead, they are limited to individual sounds, or calls. But whether a bird sings or calls, communication is part of avian life.

On an island off the coast of Peru, a blue-footed booby displays its fanciest foot-work in a courtship dance. At the start of the mating season, a booby pair dances together, rocking from side to side and slowly lifting their feet.

Biology and Behavior

The wandering albatross spends most of its life far from land, soaring over the open ocean. Once this bird takes to the air, months may pass before it touches down on solid earth. During its time at sea, the albatross roves over great distances. It feeds on fish and squids that it finds, alive or dead, on the surface of the sea. It eats garbage, too, that is thrown off ships.

The wingspan of the albatross is the widest of any bird, up to 12 feet (3.7 m) from wingtip to wingtip. Yet during its long flights the albatross rarely flaps those huge wings. Most of the time, the wind alone lifts the bird so that it can sail on the currents of the air. The albatross does not even have to use its muscles to hold its wings open. It has an energy-saving device built into its skeleton—an arrangement like a catch or lock in its wingbones holds the wings open without effort.

The albatross is magnificently adapted to the life of a sky wanderer. Among the birds, biology and behavior have evolved to suit many other ways of life as well.

PARTS OF A BIRD

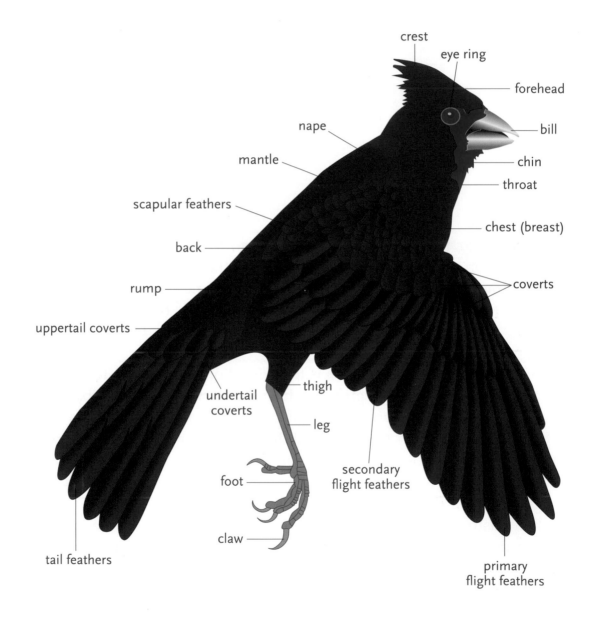

crest

eye ring

forehead

nape

bill

mantle

chin

throat

scapular feathers

chest (breast)

back

coverts

rump

uppertail coverts

thigh

undertail
coverts

leg

foot

secondary
flight feathers

claw

tail feathers

primary
flight feathers

DISTINCTIVE PHYSICAL FEATURES

Ornithologists define birds in many ways, but the simplest definition is this: "If it has feathers, it's a bird." Birds are the only living things with feathers, and all birds have feathers on at least some parts of their bodies. But what exactly is a feather?

Feathers are made of a protein called keratin. They are a specialized form of reptile scales. (Birds have scales, too, on their feet, legs, and sometimes other featherless parts of their bodies.) Different kinds of feathers serve different purposes. Flight feathers on a bird's tail and wings provide lift for flying. Sleek contour feathers streamline the bird's silhouette and provide

Flamingoes' coloration ranges from white to deep pink. The color of the feathers comes from pigments called carotenoids in the flamingoes' primary foods, which are algae and tiny shrimplike crustaceans.

How Birds Fly

"Write of swimming underwater, and you will have the flight of birds through the air." Those words were written sometime between 1488 and 1505 by the Italian scientist and artist Leonardo da Vinci.

Leonardo spent years watching birds in flight, seeking to understand the "science of the winds." He drew plans for many flying machines, including one that he called the "great bird." Also known as an ornithopter, it had two huge wings made of cloth stretched over reed frameworks, with a platform hanging beneath them. The flier would rest on this platform and flap the wings by using his feet to work a system of cords and pulleys. In his notes, Leonardo suggested testing the great bird over water, in case of a crash.

There is no record that Leonardo ever built one of his flying machines. To this day, in fact, no one has built a human-powered machine that flies just like a bird. We have, however, learned *how* birds fly. The principles of aerodynamics, the science of how air behaves and how it affects objects in the air, are the basis of flight for both birds and airplanes.

Anything that flies must overcome two forces, gravity and drag. Gravity is the force that pulls everything down toward the earth. Drag is the resistance of the air against something moving forward through it. Fliers counteract gravity with an upward force called lift, and they counteract drag with a forward force called thrust. For birds, the key to both lift and thrust is the shape of the wing when seen from the side. It is a teardrop shape, deeper in front than in back, that aerodynamics experts call an airfoil.

As a bird flies, the leading edge, or front, of its wing encounters air resistance. The air flows around the wing on top and bottom, but the airfoil shape spreads the currents of air out a little as they flow over the top. The air currents that pass under the wing, in contrast, are compressed, or pushed together. As a result the air pressure below the wing is slightly higher than normal, while that above the wing is slightly lower. The difference in air pressure creates lift, allowing the bird to rise.

Birds and airplanes also need thrust, the power that drives them forward. In planes, while the wing creates lift, the propellors or jet engines provide thrust. In birds, the wing does both. It creates lift and also acts as a propellor, providing thrust through the wingstroke. The motion of the wingstroke is not an up-and-down flap—it is a rotation, in which the wing moves forward and back in a small circle. As the wing comes forward on the downstroke, the leading edge of the wing is lower than the trailing edge, or rear. On the upstroke, the wing moves slightly back. In other words, as a bird flies, its wings scoop the air and push it to the rear. The faster the bird can do this, the more thrust it creates, and the faster it flies. To slow down, the bird simply slows its wingbeat. To land, it stalls, rotating its wings backward so that the leading edge points up. This acts as a brake. The bird may create a second brake by pointing its tail downward and fanning its tail feathers.

Wingbeats create thrust, but birds can move through the air—sometimes for hours or even days—without beating their wings often. If the air is moving, all a bird has to do is spread its wings and glide. At sea, birds glide on trade winds. On land, they harness the updrafts that occur when air currents meet buildings and hills. Birds also float on thermals, masses of air that rise through the atmosphere because they are warm. If you see a hawk or vulture circling lazily over a field on a sunny day, it is riding a thermal, just as Leonardo da Vinci wished to do.

An Arctic tern is ready to launch into flight.

some waterproofing. Short, soft down feathers beneath the contour feathers keep birds warm by trapping body heat. Plumes are ornamental feathers, often long and sometimes curled. Bristles are short stiff feathers around the eyes and bills of some birds; they can look like eyebrows or mustaches.

A bird's coloring is caused by pigments in its feathers. Some birds' coloring changes over their lifetimes, or with the passing seasons, as the feathers change. Feathers are fragile. They get dull, worn, or damaged and must be replaced. In a process called molting, old feathers fall out—usually one or two at a time, not all at once—and new ones grow up through the follicles, or openings in the bird's skin. Birds typically molt once or twice a year.

PARTS OF A FEATHER

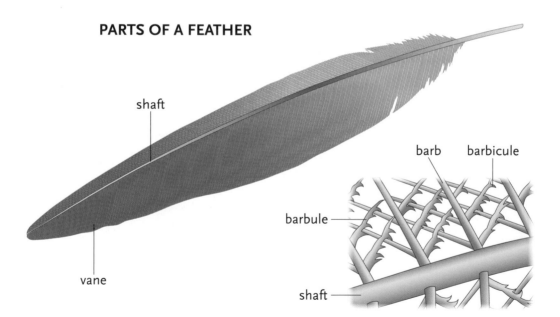

Feathers evolved first for insulation, later for flying. Flight feathers must be smooth, to cut down air resistance. The barbs that make up a feather's vane are lined with smaller branching structures called barbules. Hook-shaped barbicules on the barbules lock onto the barbules of the neighboring barb. This keeps the barbs lined up and the vane flat.

Birds are the only animals that have air sacs attached to their lungs and even inside some of their bones. When a bird draws air into its lungs, the sacs also fill with air. When the bird breathes out, air from the sacs flows back into the lungs. This gives the bird a constant supply of oxygen, even when it is emptying its lungs. The air sacs also help make birds light and buoyant.

BIRD SKELETON

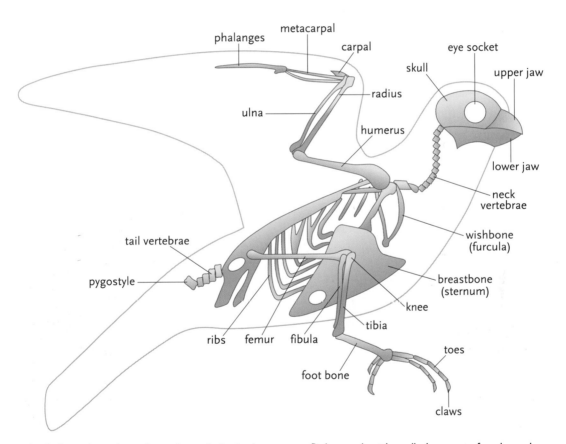

A bird's breastbone has a big ridge called a keel to support flight muscles. The collarbones are fused together for extra strength, forming the wishbone. The bones of a bird's leg and foot are much like those of mammals and reptiles, while the wing bones are adapted from arm bones. The pygostyle evolved from the vertebrae of the long bony tails of some dinosaurs and reptiles. It controls the movement of the bird's tail feathers.

Most birds do not have very good senses of smell. Vultures are one exception—they follow their noses to sun-baked roadkill and other food sources. Other birds find food chiefly by using their extremely keen senses of sight. Birds are very good at seeing sudden motions that might indicate a predator, or prey. They are also good at seeing color, but they do not see it exactly as people do. Scientists have discovered that birds can see ultraviolet light, which is beyond the limits of human vision. Ultraviolet light adds a dimension to birds' perception of color, but because humans cannot see it, we will never know, for example, how a flower looks to a hummingbird.

THE LIFE CYCLE

Birds' mating, nesting, and parenting habits are as varied as everything else about this large class of animals. Still, the stages in the life cycle are common to all birds.

Two male frigate birds inflate their throat patches to attract the attention of a female. Like many other bird species, frigate birds have a quality that scientists call sexual dichromatism, which means that males and females have different coloring.

Mating usually happens at a specific time of year, the mating season. Each species has its own mating season, timed so that the chicks will hatch and grow up during a season of plentiful food and favorable weather. Some birds mate with multiple partners. About nine-tenths of all species, though, form monogamous pairs in which the male and female stay together for the mating season or longer. Many kinds of birds, such as swans and penguins, are said to "mate for life." This is true, in the sense that pairs stay together for a lifetime. But researchers have found that many birds in these lifetime pairs also have sexual encounters with other birds.

All birds are oviparous, which means that they lay eggs from which their young hatch. Not all birds, however, build nests to hold their eggs. Some, including some shorebirds and nightbirds, simply lay their eggs in hollows on the ground or forks in tree branches. Chicks of these species are usually born with downy feathers and can see and walk as soon as they

Male bowerbirds weave large nests called bowers and decorate them with colorful objects. Different species of bowerbirds have different color schemes. A female may examine a dozen or more bowers before choosing her mate.

hatch. Other species build nests out of many kinds of materials—pebbles, branches, clay, mounds of vegetation, leaves, and miscellaneous materials such as cast-off snakeskins and bits of paper or string. The nests are used only to house eggs and young, however. Adult birds may have regular roosts, such as holes in trees, but they do not typically sleep in nests.

Perching birds build snugly woven nests of twigs and grasses to hold their eggs and house their feeble chicks. The passerines also incubate their eggs and chicks, as do birds in many other orders. Males often help with incubation. One well-known case involves male emperor penguins, who spend the brutally cold Antarctic winters holding their eggs and chicks on

The ostrich's eggs are the largest of any living bird species. The average egg weighs about 2.75 pounds (1.24 kilograms), more than twenty times as much as an average hen's egg.

Hungry young northern flickers emerge from their nest cavity to greet their father. The male flicker has fed on insects and grubs and will feed his young by regurgitating partly digested food into their mouths.

their feet, incubating them in folds of belly skin.

Bird eggs are hard-shelled. To hatch, a bird embryo must break out of its egg. It does this by pecking a hole from inside with its egg tooth, a sharp growth on its upper bill that disappears soon after hatching. The time between hatching and fledging, or leaving the nest, varies from ten days or a couple of weeks for most perching birds to about ten months for the king penguins. During that time, the young birds are fed by their parents.

Once young birds fledge, they may be independent, or they may stay with their parents and continue to receive some parental care and protection while they learn to find food and prepare to live on their own. When the young bird has reached adulthood, it will begin the cycle of mating and rearing young of its own.

Scientists do not yet know how long most species of birds live in the wild. They do know that the lifespans of wild birds are usually shorter than those of captive birds. Small wild birds typically live from two or three years to eight or ten. Larger birds have longer lifespans—twenty-five years for the bald eagle, for example. Parrots are the longest-lived birds. African gray parrots and some macaws have a maximum lifespan of sixty years or more.

MIGRATION

Birds that live in places where the weather and food supply are pretty much the same all year do not migrate, or move from one location to another and back again as the seasons change. For about half of all bird

The mud flats of the Copper River Delta in Alaska are a resting-point for western sandpipers on their spring migration. Scientists estimate that up to 6.5 million migrating sandpipers pass through the delta in just a few weeks each spring.

species, though, migration is a main event of life. Some tropical birds migrate to escape seasonal droughts or the heavy rains called monsoons, but the majority of migrating birds live in northern North America and Eurasia during the summer. When fall comes, they fly south to spend the winter in warmer, more hospitable locations where more food can be found. In the spring, they return north. Migration is demanding and dangerous. Some experts estimate that almost half of all migrating birds perish along the way. With such a high cost, migration is a good strategy only for species that would face even higher losses if they did not migrate.

Birds of many species share the same migration routes, which are called flyways. At certain times of the year, these flyways are filled with flocks of geese, ducks, songbirds, cranes, hawks, and other migrators. Each species flies at a characteristic height, and each stops to eat, drink, and rest at the same spots along the route each year. Lakes and fields that are almost empty of birds in midsummer or midwinter may be blanketed with tens of thousands of birds in the spring or fall, as migrating flocks stop to refuel.

Ornithologists think that birds follow their migration routes by using a combination of senses. They see and recognize landmarks such as coastlines and islands. They tell direction by the sun and perhaps by the stars at night. Birds are also thought to be able to sense patterns in the earth's magnetic field, which acts as a sort of map.

The world champion migrator is the *Sterna paradisaea*, the Arctic tern. This middle-sized shorebird's home range is in eastern North America from Maine to the Arctic. Each fall, it flies southeast across the Atlantic Ocean to the coast of Europe. Continuing south, the tern flies along the African coast, then to the edge of Antarctica, where it feeds on fish during the Antarctic summer. On its return, the Arctic tern flies north along the coast of South America, back across the Atlantic to Europe, and then northwest to its home range. In the course of this round trip, which can be as long as 22,000 miles (35,200 km), the tern passes through the eastern, western, northern, and southern hemispheres.

Alone or Together?

Birds' social lives range from nonexistent to overwhelming. Some birds are solitary, spending all of their time alone except when mating and raising young. Most owls fall into this category. Some birds that are normally solitary may form small groups when they migrate. Goshawks are one example.

Many species regularly gather into feeding flocks. These may range from several dozen black-capped chickadees working their way through the treetops to several thousand seed-eating grackles swarming over a freshly planted field. *Progne subis,* or the purple martin, is one of many birds that are colonial roosters, passing the night clustered together in groups.

Penguins and some shorebirds and wading birds nest wing to wing in large crowded, noisy colonies. For example, colonies of gannets and boobies may number in the millions of individuals. Scarlet ibises not only breed in colonies, they feed and roost that way, too, and are never apart from the group. One benefit of colonial living is increased safety from predators. A single bird amid a hundred thousand or a million others has much less risk of being snatched up by a predator than one bird that is feeding or nesting on its own.

Purple martins and tree swallows share a perch. Members of similar species, such as martins and swallows, sometimes feed and roost in mixed flocks.

Cool, mossy conifer forests are the summer habitat of the dark-eyed junco, a member of the sparrow family that feeds on seeds and insects picked from the forest floor.

Not all migrations are as heroic as the Arctic tern's. Some birds migrate locally. In Oregon, *Junco hyemalis,* the dark-eyed junco, likes to spend the spring and summer breeding season in cool fir forests on the slopes of the Cascade Mountains. In winter, many juncos move down to lower elevations, where temperatures are milder, to forage in woodlands and brushy fields. Like many other small birds, juncos have learned to make use of another resource—backyard birdfeeders, crumbs and corn scattered on the ground, and other treats provided by the millions of people who enjoy seeing and feeding wild birds.

A man fishes with trained cormorants in the Li River in southern China. Since ancient times Asians have used cormorants to catch fish. A ring around each bird's neck prevents it from swallowing the fish, but it is rewarded with a share of the day's catch.

CHAPTER FOUR

People and Birds

Imagine how amazing it would be to see a giant moa, larger than any bird now alive. Or imagine witnessing a cloud of passenger pigeons flying over the midwestern United States, so many millions of birds that they darkened the sky for minutes at a time, as they did during the nineteenth century. These birds did not become extinct a long time ago through natural causes, like *Archaeopteryx*. They and some other species vanished recently, hunted to the last bird.

Overhunting remains a threat to many species of birds, but other threats exist. All of the most serious problems birds face today are caused by human activity. Still, there is hope that just as people have created grave threats to many kinds of birds, they can work together to solve problems and save species.

CRISIS AND CONSERVATION

In 2006, an association of international biology and conservation groups called the World Conservation Union (IUCN) reported that of the 9,934

Parrots are crammed into a small cage and exposed to punishing heat at a roadside stand in India, despite local laws against such mistreatment. The trade in birds often skirts the law—or breaks it outright—and includes many cruel practices.

bird species it had evaluated, 1,206 were either endangered (at risk of extinction) or threatened (at risk of becoming endangered). In other words, 12 percent of the world's bird species were in trouble.

One source of trouble is people killing birds for food or sport, or capturing them for the pet trade. Many nations now try to regulate the kinds of birds that can be hunted, as well as the number that can be killed. The capture of wild birds for trade, however, is a growing problem because many of the most desirable birds are the rarest and most endangered. Trade in such birds is illegal, but it continues all the same. Anyone thinking of buying a bird as a pet should make certain that it was born in captivity or taken from a sustainable population.

Pet cats, windows, and cars kill many times more birds a year than hunters do. Some researchers into bird populations think that uncontrolled domestic cats alone are the single most destructive human-caused threat to birds. Cats are estimated to be responsible for a billion or more bird deaths each year. Another 80 million birds die from injuries caused by crashing into glass windows, which are hard for them to see, or communication wires and towers.

Another human activity that has had grim consequences for birds is our practice of introducing animals to places where they do not occur naturally. The southern Pacific islands of New Zealand are a classic example of the dangers of introduced species. New Zealand is home to many unusual bird species that evolved in isolation there. Many of them are slow-moving ground dwellers that flourished without many predators. When Europeans settled the islands, they introduced dogs, cats, and rats. These new predators wiped out some species of native birds and have threated many more. People introduced weasels to the islands, hoping these would control the rat population, but the weasels have made matters worse—now there are more predators killing endangered birds such as *Strigops habroptilus,* the kakapo, and *Porphyrio mantelli,* the takahe. Even the various species of kiwi, New Zealand's national symbol, are endangered. The same thing has happened in Hawaii, where the nene goose, the state bird, has dwindled to just a few hundred individuals and needs constant protection from pigs and other introduced predators.

Pollution of air, water, and food sources such as fish is another serious threat to birds.

A pair of takahe forage for food beneath the sign that tells visitors to this New Zealand wildlife sanctuary about the imperiled species.

From oil spills to pesticides and heavy metals in water, things that are bad for birds are generally bad for other living things in the environment, including people. Governments have taken steps toward reducing environmental pollution—for example, many countries have banned the pesticide DDT, which was absorbed by birds and led to defective eggs. Yet lead, mercury, and oil are on the rise in the environment. These toxic materials reduce birds' ability to breed and develop properly.

One of the most widespread threats to birds and many other forms of life is habitat loss. Every day, around the world, tropical forests are cut, wetlands are bulldozed for development, housing is built on coastlines,

Human trash is a major threat to birds such as these albatross on a Hawaiian beach. Birds evolved to snatch small things out of the water. Today, though, many things that look like fish are really bottles or plastic bags. Dead seabirds have been found with their stomachs full of the plastic junk that killed them.

Burrowing owls, the only ground-dwelling owls, nest in abandoned rodent holes and tunnels. Once common in America's open grasslands, they are now endangered or at risk in many areas.

and prairies, scrubland, and woods are plowed into farmland. One of the greatest challenges conservationists face is finding a way to balance human needs with those of the rest of the natural world, including birds. Many birds are so perfectly adapted to their environments—including the environments where they spend their migrations—that they cannot move to different regions or habitats. If the habitat disappears, so does the bird.

For the nene goose and many others, the only hope of long-term survival may lie in zoos, captive breeding programs, or round-the-clock protection. Governments, scientists, and conservationists have made intense and costly efforts to save some species, such as the California condor, that have reached the edge of extinction. But such efforts cannot be made for all threatened species. What will their fate be?

BACK FROM EXTINCTION?

The ivory-billed woodpecker once lived in river forests across the southeastern United States. It was one of the biggest woodpeckers in the world,

The only ivory-billed woodpeckers that most people have seen are stuffed museum specimens like this one. Since 2004, however, a few searchers may have caught glimpses of living birds in the swamp forest of Arkansas.

American naturalist John James Audubon painted these ivory-billed woodpeckers around 1830, a century before the species vanished.

sometimes measuring more than 19 inches (48 cm) in length, with broad white patches on its black wings and an upward-pointing crest of feathers—red on male birds, black on females—on the top of its head. The woodpecker ate beetles and grubs that it dug out of the bark of dead and dying trees with the long, strong, white bill that was the source of its name.

Because ivory-billed woodpeckers were large, handsome, and also rather rare, bird collectors clamored for them. Between the 1890s and the 1920s, professional collectors took a heavy toll on the species. An even bigger blow to the woodpecker's survival was the clearing of millions of acres of old forest in the river valleys and wet bottomlands of the Southeast. As the habitat of the ivory-billed woodpecker disappeared, so did the bird. By the late 1930s, the only known surviving population of the woodpeckers lived in a forested area of northern Louisiana called the Singer Tract. Then, in spite of protests from conservationists, the Singer Tract was logged. The last definite sighting of an ivory-billed woodpecker in the United States was in 1944. A related population of ivory-billed woodpeckers was known to live in Cuba, just south of Florida. The last confirmed sightings there took place in the 1950s, although a few researchers claimed to see ivory-billed woodpeckers in Cuba in the 1980s.

For generations there have been rumors of ivory-billed woodpeckers being spotted in the Southeast. None of these claims, however, could be considered proof. Many birders dreamed of finding hidden survivors of the species and proving beyond all doubt that the ivory-billed woodpecker still existed. On February 11, 2004, Gene Sparling thought he had succeeded.

Sparling was kayaking alone through the Cache River National Wildlife Refuge in Arkansas when he spotted a very large red-crested woodpecker. He hinted on his Web site that it had looked like an ivory-billed wood-pecker. One of those who read Sparling's account was Tim Gallagher of Cornell University's Laboratory of Ornithology. A few weeks after Sparling's original sighting, Sparling led Gallagher and another scientist to the place where he had seen the bird. They saw it, too, and were convinced it was an ivory-billed woodpecker. Over the following year, there were five more sightings. One observer captured the bird on video for a few seconds. Although the image is blurred and indistinct, Gallagher and a group of colleagues believe that it shows an ivory-billed woodpecker and not a pileated woodpecker, another large bird that is common in the area. Other experts, however, point out that while the bird *could* have been an ivory-billed woodpecker, the identification cannot be called definite. The bottom line is that although many people think that Sparling and others have seen ivory-billed woodpeckers, as of early 2007 this had not been proven.

Since 2004, the U.S. Fish and Wildlife Service, with partners from several universities and wildlife-management agencies, has formed a Recovery Team to search for ivory-billed woodpeckers in Arkansas and elsewhere, and to protect the bird and its habitat if its existence is confirmed. The researchers are haunted by questions: Did Sparling and others really see an ivory-billed woodpecker in 2004-2005? If so, was it part of a small breeding population, or was it a single bird without a mate, perhaps the last of its kind? Finally, if the ivory-billed woodpecker *is* hanging on in the depths of some southeastern forests, can the species recover?

One encouraging fact is that conservation practices over the past half century have brought back some of the mature river and swamp forest that is the ivory-billed woodpecker's habitat. Perhaps in years to come the bird will once again occupy this habitat. "Nature gives very few second chances," said Carter Roberts, president of the World Wildlife Fund, when the possible rediscovery of the ivory-billed woodpecker was announced. "This is one of them."

Birds have fascinated and inspired people throughout human history. Now it is time for people to protect threatened birds and their habitats, so that the diversity of the bird class—the last living dinosaurs—continues into the future.

Reddish egrets, once hunted almost to extinction so that their plumes could be used on women's hats, are now protected from hunting in the United States. But they face a new threat—the loss of their breeding grounds, which are wetlands and lagoons around the Gulf of Mexico. Conservationists in Florida and Texas have set up preserves so that these birds, North America's rarest herons, may survive.

adapt—To change or develop in ways that aid survival in the environment.

anatomy—Physical structure.

ancestral—Having to do with lines of descent or earlier forms.

arboreal—Tree-dwelling.

avian—Having to do with birds.

conservation—Action or movement aimed at protecting and preserving wildlife or its habitat.

crepuscular—Active by dusk or evening.

diurnal—Active by day.

evolution—The pattern of change in life forms over time, as new species, or types of plants and animals, develop from old ones.

evolve—To change over time.

extinct—No longer existing; died out.

genetic—Having to do with genes, material made of DNA inside the cells of living organisms. Genes carry information about inherited characteristics from parents to offspring and determine the form of each organism.

incubate—To keep eggs at the proper temperature for development, often by sitting on them.

migration—Seasonal movement of animals, sometimes in large groups, between two territories or locations.

nectar—Sugary liquid produced inside many flowers.

nocturnal—Active by night.

ornithology—The scientific study of birds.

paleontology—The study of ancient life, mainly through fossils.

pesticide—Something that kills organisms that humans regard as pests.

plumage—Feathers.

taxonomy—Scientific system for classifying living things, grouping them in categories according to similarities and differences, and naming them.

terrestrial—Living on the ground.

vertebrate—An animal with a backbone.

BIRD

CLASS

SUBCLASS

Extinct birds

SUPERORDER

INFRAORDER

Neoaves

23 ORDERS

Sphenisciformes (penguins)
Gaviiformes (loons)
Procellariiformes (tube-nosed seabirds)
Falconiformes (birds of prey)
Podicipediformes (grebes)
Phoenicopteriformes (flamingoes)
Charadriiformes (shorebirds and relatives)
Pelecaniformes (pelicans, cormorants, and relatives)
Ciconiiformes (storks, herons, ibises)
Gruiformes (cranes, rails, coots)
Strigiformes (owls)
Caprimulgiformes (nightbirds)
Apodiformes (hummingbirds and swifts)
Musophagiformes (turacos)
Opisthocomiformes (hoatzin)
Columbiformes (doves and pigeons)
Psittaciformes (parrots)
Cuculiformes (cuckoos)
Piciformes (woodpeckers, toucans, honeyguides, and relatives)
Coraciiformes (kingfishers and relatives)
Trogoniformes (trogons)
Coliiformes (mousebirds)
Passeriformes (perching birds, many families)

ORDER

FAMILY TREE

Aves (Birds)

Neornithes (modern birds)

Neognathae

Paleognathae

Galloanserae

2 ORDERS

Galliformes (chickens, grouse, quail, pheasants, and relatives)
Anseriformes (ducks, geese, swans, and relatives)

2 ORDERS

Tinamiformes (tinamous)
Struthioniformes (ratites: ostrich, emus, rheas, cassowaries, kiwis)

F U R T H E R   R E A D I N G

Arnold, Caroline. *Birds: Nature's Magnificent Flying Machines.* Watertown, MA: Charlesbridge, 2003.

Brinkley, Edward S. *Birds.* Pleasantville, NY: Reader's Digest, 2000.

Dubois, Philippe and Valerie Guidoux. *Birds.* New York: Abrams, 2005.

Gray, Samantha and Sarah Walker. *Birds.* New York: Dorling Kindersley, 2002.

Hickman, Pamela. *Birds of Prey Rescue: Changing the Future for Endangered Wildlife.* Richmond Hill, Ontario: Firefly, 2006.

Solway, Andrew. *Birds of Prey.* Chicago: Heinemann, 2005.

Stefoff, Rebecca. *Penguins.* Tarrytown, NY: Benchmark, 2005.

Warhol, Tom and Chris Reiter. *Eagles.* Tarrytown, NY: Benchmark, 2003.

Warhol, Tom. *Hawks.* Tarrytown, NY: Benchmark, 2005.

Weidensaul, Scott. *National Audubon Society First Field Guide to Birds.* New York: Scholastic, 1998.

WEB SITES

http://animaldiversity.ummz.umich.edu/site/accounts/information/
Aves.html
The Birds section of the Animal Diversity Web, maintained by the University of Michigan Museum of Zoology, has pages on bird classification and on many bird families.

http://www.tolweb.org/Aves/15721
The Aves section of the Tree of Life Web Project has pages on bird evolution, extinct groups of avian ancestors, and modern birds, with many links to other Web resources.

http://www.enchantedlearning.com/subject/birds/
This All About Birds site has summaries of bird evolution and biology, along with a list of the birds that are symbols of the American states, the Canadian provinces, and many countries around the world.

http://www.enchantedlearning.com/subjects/dinosaurs/Dinobirds.html
This page is called Dinosaurs and Birds; it explores the evolutionary link between the ancient dinosaurs and modern birds, with brief descriptions of important fossils.

http://www.birds.cornell.edu/AllAboutBirds/
The All About Birds site of Cornell University's Laboratory of Ornithology is a good introduction to birdwatching and bird conservation.

http://www.ucmp.berkeley.edu/vertebrates/flight/aves.html
How birds fly is the subject of this Avian Flight page, maintained by the University of California Museum of Paleontology.

http://www.nhm.org/birds/home.html
> The Bird site of the Natural History Museum of Los Angeles County has easy-to-read material for students on bird evolution, biology, flight, and conservation.

http://www.explorebiodiversity.com/bird.htm
> Called The Life of Birds, this site has short but informative sections on birds of the world (including videos of some living species), adaptations (such as feeding and flight), ecology, reproduction, and behaviors (such as migration and singing).

http://www.enature.com/fieldguides/intermediate.asp?curGroupID=1
> The National Wildlife Federation's eNature site offers a photographic guide to bird species found in North America, as well as articles on birdwatching.

http://www.pbs.org/wgbh/nova/sciencenow/3302/03.html
> This page from PBS's Nova site gives a good overview of the hunt for the ivory-billed woodpecker, in the form of questions and answers with an ornithologist and a biologist.

http://www.bsc-eoc.org/links/
> Bird Links to the World is a well-organized collection of thousands of links to resources that include a database of pictures and sound recordings of birds, field trip reports by birders around the world, and dozens of sites concerned with bird conservation, bird biology, and birdwatching.

http://animals.about.com/od/onlinecourse1/a/birdsupclose.htm
> About.com's site Birds: A Study Guide offers brief overviews of flight, migration, and bird classification, with links to additional resources and a glossary of bird terms.

B I B L I O G R A P H Y

The author found these sources very helpful when researching this book.

Alsop, Fred. *Smithsonian Birds of North America.* New York: DK Publishing, 2006.

Attenborough, David. *The Life of Birds.* Princeton, NJ: Princeton University Press, 1998.

Beletsky, Les. *Birds of the World.* Baltimore, MD: Johns Hopkins University Press, 2006.

Burger, Joanna. *Birds: A Visual Guide.* Buffalo, NY: Firefly Books, 2006.

Carrano, Matthew T. and Patrick M. O'Connor. "Bird's-Eye View." *Natural History,* Vol. 114, Number 4, May 2005, pp. 42-47.

Clements, James F. *Birds of the World: A Checklist.* 5th edition. Vista, CA: Ibis Publishing, 2000.

Cornell Laboratory of Ornithology. *Handbook of Bird Biology.* Princeton, NJ: Princeton University Press, 2004.

Gallagher, Tim. *The Grail Bird: The Rediscovery of the Ivory-Billed Woodpecker.* Reprint edition. Boston: Houghton Mifflin, 2006.

Gibson, Graeme. *The Bedside Book of Birds: An Avian Miscellany.* New York: Nan A. Talese/Doubleday, 2005.

Lemonick, Michael D. "Dinosaur Tales." Time, October 25, 2004, pp. 74-75.

Rotherberg, David. *Why Birds Sing: A Journey into the Mystery of Bird Song.* New York: Perseus Books, 2006.

Short, Lester L. *The Lives of Birds: Birds of the World and Their Behavior.* New York: Henry Holt, 1993.

Sibley, David. *The Sibley Guide to Bird Life and Behavior.* London: Christopher Helm, 2001.

I N D E X

Page numbers in **boldface** are illustrations.

Rebecca Stefoff is the author of a number of books on scientific subjects for young readers. She has explored the world of plants and animals in Marshall Cavendish's Living Things series and in several volumes of the AnimalWays series, also published by Marshall Cavendish. For the Family Trees series, she has authored books on primates, flowering plants, amphibians, birds, marsupials, and fungi. Stefoff has also written about evolution in *Charles Darwin and the Evolution Revolution* (Oxford University Press, 1996), and she appeared in the *A&E Biography* program on Darwin and his work. Stefoff lives in Portland, Oregon. You can learn more about her and her books at www.rebeccastefoff.com.